Premier dictionnaire illustré
Animaux

First Picture Dictionary
Animals

Cochon
Pig

Lapin
Rabbit

Papillon
Butterfly

Renard
Fox

Illustré par Anna Ivanir

www.kidkiddos.com
Copyright ©2025 by KidKiddos Books Ltd.
support@kidkiddos.com

All rights reserved. No part of this book may be reproduced in any form or by any electronic or mechanical means, including information storage and retrieval systems, without written permission from the publisher, except in the case of a reviewer, who may quote brief passages embodied in critical articles or in a review.
First edition, 2025

Library and Archives Canada Cataloguing in Publication
First Picture Dictionary – Animals (French English Bilingual edition)
ISBN: 978-1-83416-300-0 paperback
ISBN: 978-1-83416-301-7 hardcover
ISBN: 978-1-83416-299-7 eBook

Animaux sauvages
Wild Animals

Lion
Lion

Tigre
Tiger

Girafe
Giraffe

Éléphant
Elephant

✦ *La girafe est l'animal terrestre le plus grand.*
✦ A giraffe is the tallest animal on land.

Singe
Monkey

Animaux sauvages
Wild Animals

Hippopotame
Hippopotamus

Panda
Panda

Renard
Fox

Rhinocéros
Rhino

Cerf
Deer

Élan
Moose

Loup
Wolf

✦ Un élan est un excellent nageur et peut plonger sous l'eau pour manger des plantes !

✦ A moose is a great swimmer and can dive underwater to eat plants!

Écureuil
Squirrel

Koala
Koala

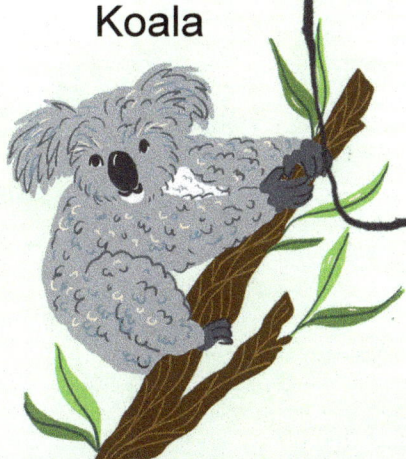

✦ Un écureuil cache des noisettes pour l'hiver, mais il oublie parfois où il les a mises !

✦ A squirrel hides nuts for winter, but sometimes forgets where it put them!

Gorille
Gorilla

Animaux de compagnie
Pets

Canari
Canary

♦ *Une grenouille peut respirer par sa peau ainsi que par ses poumons !*
♦ A frog can breathe through its skin as well as its lungs!

Cochon d'Inde
Guinea Pig

Grenouille
Frog

Hamster
Hamster

Poisson rouge
Goldfish

Chien
Dog

◆ Certains perroquets peuvent répéter des mots et même rire comme un humain !

◆ *Some parrots can copy words and even laugh like a human!*

Chat
Cat

Perroquet
Parrot

Animaux de la ferme
Animals at the Farm

Vache
Cow

Poule
Chicken

Canard
Duck

Mouton
Sheep

Cheval
Horse

Moustique
Mosquito

Libellule
Dragonfly

✦ *La libellule est l'un des premiers insectes apparus sur Terre, même avant les dinosaures !*
✦ A dragonfly was one of the first insects on Earth, even before dinosaurs!

Abeille
Bee

Papillon
Butterfly

Coccinelle
Ladybug

Blaireau
Badger

Porc-épic
Porcupine

Marmotte
Groundhog

◆ *Un lézard peut faire repousser sa queue s'il la perd !*
◆ A lizard can grow a new tail if it loses one!

Lézard
Lizard

Fourmi
Ant

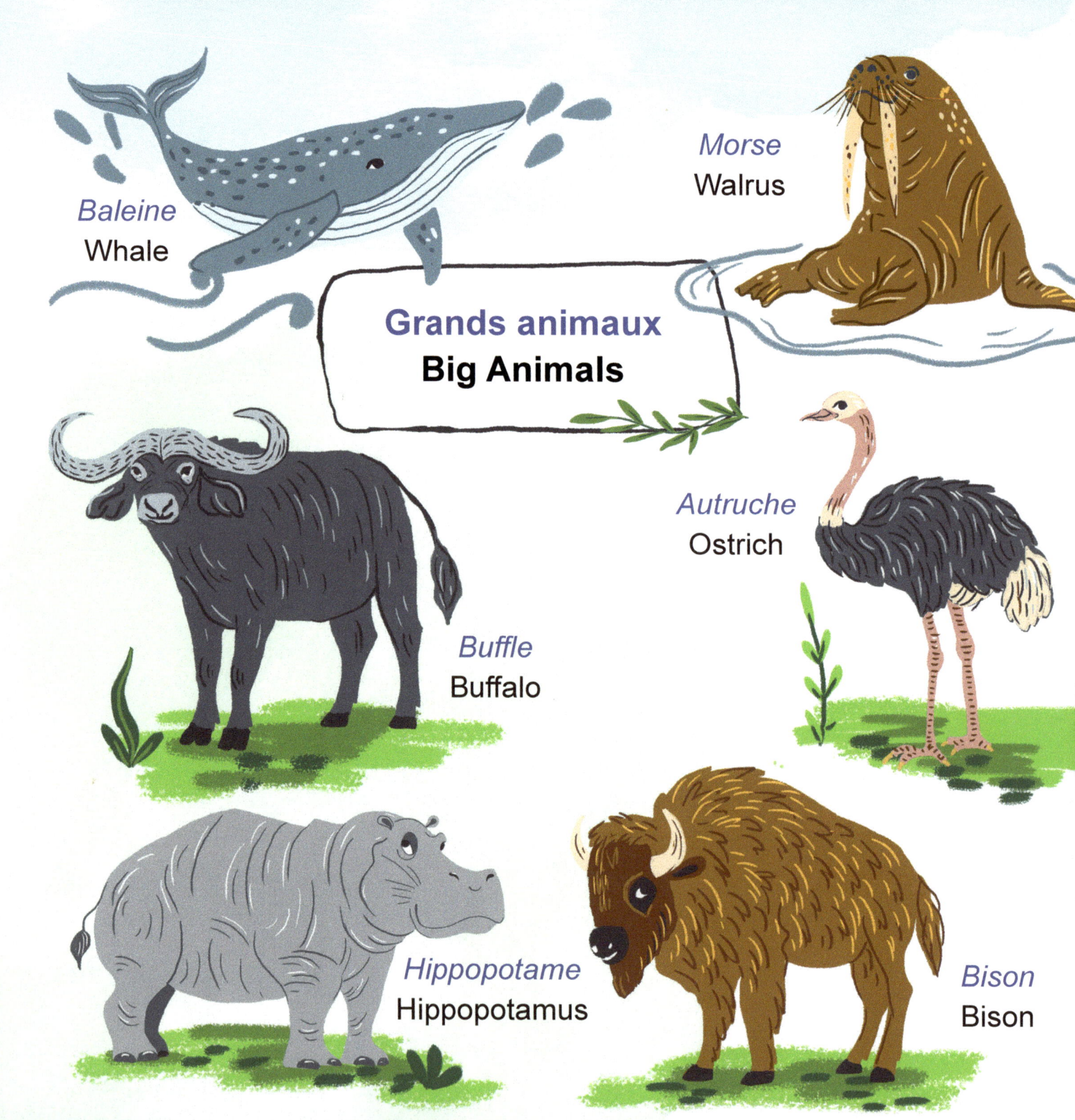

Petits animaux
Small Animals

Caméléon
Chameleon

Araignée
Spider

- *L'autruche est le plus grand oiseau, mais elle ne peut pas voler !*
- *An ostrich is the biggest bird, but it cannot fly!*

Abeille
Bee

- *Un escargot porte sa maison sur son dos et se déplace très lentement.*
- *A snail carries its home on its back and moves very slowly.*

Escargot
Snail

Souris
Mouse

Animaux silencieux
Quiet Animals

Coccinelle
Ladybug

Tortue
Turtle

◆ *Une tortue peut vivre sur terre et dans l'eau.*
◆ A turtle can live both on land and in water.

Poisson
Fish

Lézard
Lizard

Animaux nocturnes
Nighttime Animals

Luciole
Firefly

Blaireau
Badger

Kiwi
Kiwi Bird

Léopard
Leopard

Hérisson
Hedgehog

Hibou
Owl

Chauve-souris
Bat

◆ Une luciole brille la nuit pour trouver d'autres lucioles.
◆ *A firefly glows at night to find other fireflies.*

◆ Un hibou chasse la nuit et utilise son ouïe pour trouver sa nourriture !
◆ *An owl hunts at night and uses its hearing to find food!*

Raton laveur
Raccoon

Mygale
Tarantula

Animaux colorés
Colorful Animals

Le flamant est rose
A flamingo is pink

Le hibou est marron
An owl is brown

Le cygne est blanc
A swan is white

Le poulpe est violet
An octopus is purple

La grenouille est verte
A frog is green

✦ *La grenouille est verte pour se cacher parmi les feuilles.*
✦ A frog is green, so it can hide among the leaves.

L'ours polaire est blanc
A polar bear is white

Le renard est orange
A fox is orange

Le koala est gris
A koala is grey

La panthère est noire
A panther is black

Le poussin est jaune
A chick is yellow

Animaux et leurs petits
Animals and Their Babies

Vache et Veau
Cow and Calf

Chat et Chaton
Cat and Kitten

✦ *Un poussin parle à sa mère même avant d'éclore.*
✦ A chick talks to its mother even before it hatches.

Poule et Poussin
Chicken and Chick

Chien et Chiot
Dog and Puppy

Papillon et Chenille
Butterfly and Caterpillar

Mouton et Agneau
Sheep and Lamb

Cheval et Poulain
Horse and Foal

Cochon et Porcelet
Pig and Piglet

Chèvre et Chevreau
Goat and Kid

www.ingramcontent.com/pod-product-compliance
Lightning Source LLC
LaVergne TN
LVHW072003060526
838200LV00010B/274